BULLY-BUSTER BINGO

INCLUDES EIGHT COMPLETE LESSONS
PLUS
REPRODUCIBLE BINGO BOARDS & ACTIVITY SHEETS

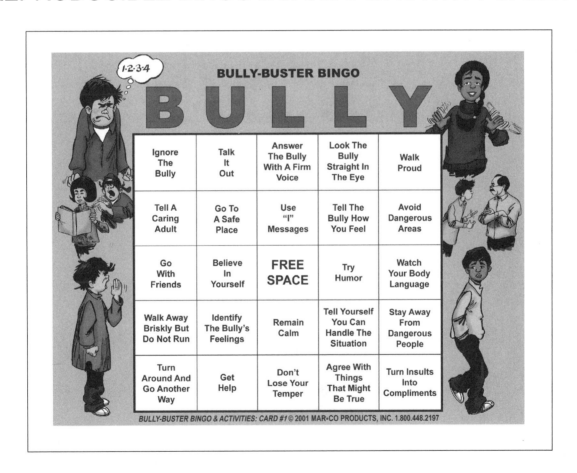

WRITTEN BY
HEIDI MCDONALD

ILLUSTRATED BY WALTER LARDNER

ABOUT THE AUTHOR

Heidi McDonald has been actively involved in education for the last 17 years. She has been employed as a middle school science, math, gifted students, and English teacher; a third- and fifth-grade teacher; and as a school guidance counselor for grades K-8 for more than eight years. Heidi McDonald received her bachelor's in Education at Arizona State University and her master's in Education at Northern Arizona University. Mrs. McDonald is currently employed by Somerton Elementary School District in Somerton, Arizona and resides in Yuma, Arizona.

Bully-Buster Bingo

10-DIGIT ISBN: 1-57543-089-4
13-DIGIT ISBN: 978-1-57543-089-8

REVISED/REPRINTED 2008
COPYRIGHT © 2001 MAR*CO PRODUCTS, INC
Published by mar*co products, inc.
1443 Old York Road
Warminster, PA 18974
1-800-448-2197
www.marcoproducts.com

PRINTED IN THE U.S.A.

CONTENTS

INTRODUCTION

Bullies represent an ever-increasing problem in today's schools. Surveys show that bullies are one of the most prevalent problems in elementary and middle schools. Young students are intimidated by kids who tease, threaten, and ostracize them. They live in fear of what will happen as they go to school each day.

No child is immune to the wrath of a bully. Any child who shows the least bit of weakness or fear or who is even slightly different is a possible target. *Bully-Buster Bingo* was written to help those children in grades 2-7 who are suffering each day, the children who hope they will never be the targets of bullies, and the bullies themselves. Bullies do not always realize the destruction their behavior causes, and for those children, this program can be helpful. Awareness of bullying behaviors and how to countermand them can also help diminish a bully's power.

Presenting lessons on bullying to an entire classroom signals the bully that everyone is aware of his/her behavior and that no one thinks very much of anyone who behaves in a bullying manner. It also gives hope to the child who is being bullied by letting him/her know that others are now aware of what is going on and do not support the bully's actions.

Bully-Buster Bingo Includes:

- 30 reproducible *Bully-Buster Bingo* game boards
- Reproducible *Bully-Buster Bingo* calling cards (one set for each letter: B, U, L, and Y)
- Reproducible *Bully-Buster Bingo* activity sheets

Presenting The Program

Reproduce the required number of *Bully-Buster Bingo* game boards (pages 36-65 or CD), a checklist (page 66 or CD), and the calling cards (pages 67-71 or CD). Cut the calling cards apart. Distribute the *Bully-Buster Bingo* game boards and chips (supplied by the leader). Each board contains 24 different techniques. Play the game by calling out the letter and technique. Students must look under the column of the letter called to find the technique that was given. If the technique appears in that column, the students may cover the square. (*Note:* There are two "L" columns on each game board. When an "L" calling card is read, students should look for the matching technique in both columns.) If the technique appears in a different column, they cannot cover the square. The leader should tell the students what must be covered before they can call out *Bully-Buster Bingo*.

When the game is over, the leader should select one or two techniques and discuss how these techniques relate to the issue of *bullying*.

Some of the techniques have been expanded into lessons. These lessons are found on pages 5-31 and can be used if the leader wishes to elaborate on the techniques. The activities are designated primary (grades 2-4) and intermediate (grades 5-7). As with any grade-level recommendations, the leader should review the contents and reading level of the activity sheet to determine its appropriateness for the students to whom it is being presented.

5

ASCA STANDARDS FOR BULLY-BUSTER BINGO

PERSONAL/SOCIAL DEVELOPMENT	DEALING WITH A BULLY	USING "I" MESSAGES	ANGRY FEELINGS	HOW DO I FEEL?	WALKING PROUD	BULLY BUSTER	BULLY LETTER	BULLYING PLAY
Standard A: Students will acquire knowledge, attitudes, and interpersonal skills to help them understand and respect self and others								
Competency A:1 Acquire Self-Knowledge								
PS/A:1.1 Develop a positive attitude toward self as a unique and worthy person					■	■	■	
PS/A:1.5 Identify and express feelings		■	■			■		
PS/A:1.6 Distinguish between appropriate and inappropriate behaviors			■	■		■	■	
PS/A:1.8 Understand the need for self-control and how to practice it			■	■				
PS/A:1.9 Demonstrate cooperative behavior in groups	■							
Competency A:2 Acquire Interpersonal Skills								
PS/A:2.6 Use effective communication skills		■	■	■	■	■		
PS/A:2.7 Know that communication involves speaking, listening, and nonverbal behavior					■	■		
Standard B: Students will make decisions, set goals, and take necessary action to achieve goals.								
Competency B:1 Self-Knowledge Applications								
PS/B:1.1 Use a decision-making and problem-solving model		■				■		
PS/B:1.4 Develop effective coping skills for dealing with problems	■					■	■	
PS/B:1.5 Demonstrate when, where, and how to seek help for solving problems and making decisions	■					■	■	
PS/B:1.6 Know how to apply conflict-resolution skills	■	■						
Standard C: Students will understand safety and survival skills.								
Competency C:1 Acquire Personal Safety Skills								
PS/C:1.6 Identify resource people in the school and community, and know how to seek their help	■					■		
PS/C:1.7 Apply effective problem-solving and decision-making skills to make safe and healthy choices	■					■	■	■
PS/C:1.10 Learn techniques for managing stress and conflict	■	■	■	■	■	■	■	■
PS/C:1.11 Learn coping skills for managing life events	■	■	■	■	■	■	■	■

DEALING WITH A BULLY
(PRIMARY AND INTERMEDIATE)

RATIONALE: Students need to plan ahead in order to deal effectively with bullies. They need to know to whom they can turn and where they can go if a problem arises with a bully. Being prepared is better and much safer than trying to think of a plan while the problem is occurring.

OBJECTIVES: The students will be able to name three caring adults to whom they can turn if they need help when dealing with a bully.

The students will be able to name three places where they can go to feel safe if threatened by a bully.

MATERIALS: For each student:
- ☐ *Bully-Buster Bingo* game board (pages 36-65 or CD)
- ☐ chips
- ☐ copy of *Dealing With A Bully* (page 8 or 9 or CD)
- ☐ crayons or pencil
- ☐ folders (optional)

For the leader:
- ☐ *Bully-Buster Bingo* calling cards

ACTIVITY: Distribute the *Bully-Buster Bingo* game boards and chips. Play a game of *Bully-Buster Bingo*. (*Note:* The center square is a "free" space.)

Begin the lesson by reminding the students that one of the important ways to deal with bullies is to know how to get help and where to go to feel safe. Ask the students to find the square on their bingo card that says *Get Help.* Explain that this phrase will not appear on all game boards and ask those students whose game boards do include it to stand. Then ask the class:

"Why do you think it would be important to get help if you were dealing with a bully?" (Allow time for answers.)

"Why do you think it would be important to know of and go to a safe place when faced with a bully?" (Allow time for answers.)

Collect the *Bully-Buster Bingo* game boards.

Distribute the activity sheet and a pencil or crayons to each student. Review the directions and tell the students to complete the assignment. When everyone has finished, allow those who wish to do so to share their answers with the group. If you decided to have the students make *Bully-Buster* Folders, tell them to place their activity sheets in their folders. If you are not using folders, allow the students to take their papers home.

NAME _____

DEALING WITH A BULLY

Remember:
When dealing with a bully, it is important to tell
a caring adult about what is going on.

Draw the faces of three caring adults you can tell if you need help.
Write each person's name on the line below the picture.

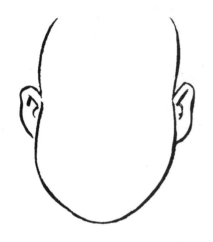 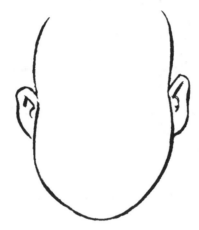 

_____ _____ _____

It is also important to have a safe place to go when
you are around a bully and don't feel safe.

Draw three places where you feel safe.

8

NAME _____

DEALING WITH A BULLY

Remember:

When dealing with a bully, it is important to tell a caring adult about what is going on.

Write the names of three caring adults in school and three caring adults at home or in your neighborhood who you can turn to if you need help:

SCHOOL:

1. _____

2. _____

3. _____

HOME OR NEIGHBORHOOD:

_____

_____

_____

It is also important to have a safe place to go when you are around a bully and don't feel safe.

Write the names of three places at school and at home or in your neighborhood where you could go for help if you do not feel safe.

SCHOOL:

1. _____

2. _____

3. _____

HOME OR NEIGHBORHOOD:

_____

_____

_____

Bully-Buster Bingo © 2001 Mar*co Products, Inc. 1.800.448.2197

USING "I" MESSAGES
(PRIMARY AND INTERMEDIATE)

RATIONALE: Students need to be able to express themselves in a way that is non-threatening to other people. They need to be able to tell how they are feeling and why they feel that way.

OBJECTIVE: The students will successfully demonstrate that they know how to use "I" messages to communicate effectively with others about how they are feeling and why they feel that way.

MATERIALS: For each student:
- ☐ *Bully-Buster Bingo* game board (pages 36-65 or CD)
- ☐ chips
- ☐ copy of *Using "I" Messages* (page 12 or 13 or CD)
- ☐ crayons or pencil
- ☐ folders (optional)

For the leader:
- ☐ *Bully-Buster Bingo* calling cards

ACTIVITY: Distribute the *Bully-Buster Bingo* game boards and chips. Play a game of *Bully-Buster Bingo*.

Begin the lesson by giving an "I" message about yourself to the class. For example:

"I feel good today because the weather is nice."

Then ask the students:

"Who was I talking about?" *(Myself)*

Explain that when you are using the word "I" with a feeling word such as *happy, sad, mad,* or *glad* you are giving an "I" message.

Ask for volunteers to make "I" messages about themselves. After the students have provided several examples of "I" messages, ask them how they could use "I" messages when somebody is bothering them. Provide those students giving examples with appropriate feedback so that the student expresses only "I" messages. For example, if someone tells a student that he/she has big ears, the feedback could be, "I do not like it when you make fun of my ears."

Explain that "I" messages are non-threatening ways of letting others, including bullies, know exactly how you feel.

Then ask the students:

"Do you think 'I' messages will work with all bullies?" *(No, because some bullies want to hurt your feelings and make you upset. When a bully doesn't care how much he/she hurts you, you might have to resort to asking for help or escaping from the situation. Other bullies don't realize how hurtful their actions can be. "I" messages may work with these bullies.)*

Then ask:

"When do you think 'I' messages will work?" *(They will work in a situation where the person making the statement is not usually a bully-type person.)*

"How many of you have *Use 'I' Messages* on your *Bully-Buster Bingo* game boards?"

Collect the *Bully-Buster Bingo* game boards and chips. Distribute *Using "I" Messages* and crayons or a pencil to each student. Review the directions and tell the students to complete the assignment. When everyone has finished, allow those who wish to do so to share their answers with the group. If you decided to have the students make *Bully-Buster* Folders, tell them to place their activity sheets in their folders. If you are not using folders, allow the students to take their papers home.

11

NAME _____

USING "I" MESSAGES

Draw a picture showing someone bullying you with words, not fists.
Write your "I" message on the line at the bottom of the page.

My "I" message is

_____

Bully-Buster Bingo © 2001 Mar★co Products, Inc. 1.800.448.2197

USING "I" MESSAGES

Remember:

It is important to let others know how you feel.
Using "I" messages will tell them exactly how you feel and why you feel that way.

Look at the cartoon below. Write in the balloon the "I" message that the boy could give.

1 "You really stink at soccer!"

2 "I don't like it when she says that.

It hurts my feelings and makes me feel sad."

3 "I feel _____ _____ when you _____ _____ _____."

WHAT I CAN DO WITH MY ANGRY FEELINGS?
(PRIMARY AND INTERMEDIATE)

RATIONALE: Students need to know how to work out problems with angry feelings in a positive way.

OBJECTIVES: The students will learn how to work out problems with angry feelings in a positive way.

The students will name at least two things that they can do if they feel angry when someone is bullying them.

MATERIALS: For each student:
- □ *Bully-Buster Bingo* game board (pages 36-65 or CD)
- □ chips
- □ copy of *What I Can Do With My Angry Feelings?* (page 16 or CD)
- □ pencil
- □ folders (optional)

For the leader:
- □ *Bully-Buster Bingo* calling cards
- □ chalkboard and chalk

ACTIVITY: Distribute the *Bully-Buster Bingo* game boards and chips. Play a game of *Bully-Buster Bingo*.

Begin the lesson by asking the students:

"What sort of things might make you feel angry?" *(Accept any appropriate answer.)*

Allow the students to brainstorm this question. Write their responses on the chalkboard. When the students have named some things that other people have done to them, circle the words that describe the types of behavior a bully might use, such as hitting, pushing, calling names, teasing, etc.

Then ask:

"Are these the type of things bullies might do if they wanted you to feel upset?" *(Yes.)*

Explain to the students that while they cannot stop other people from bullying them, there are things they can do to help themselves feel better when they are picked on.

Then ask:

"Can anyone tell me something you could do to make yourself feel better if you were angry about being bullied?"

14

Write the students' answers on the chalkboard, making sure that all suggestions from the bingo game boards are included as well as the following suggestions: running, taking a walk, visiting a friend, playing a game, riding a bike, jumping up and down, writing in a journal, reading a book, talking it out, telling a caring adult, writing a letter to the person you are angry with and throwing it away. For each suggestion, have the student tell why the activity would help him/her get rid of angry feelings.

Have the students look at their *Bully-Buster Bingo* game boards. Tell them to look for things they could do to handle their angry feelings. Some of the answers could be: ignore the bully, talk it out, walk away, answer with a firm voice, tell a caring adult, try humor, get help, and remain calm. Have the students explain the reasons for their answers.

When you have finished the activity, tell the students:

> "Remember that being angry is not a bad thing. *Anger* is a feeling, and feelings are never bad or wrong. It is only the way you react to a feeling that might not be helpful. For example, when kids use violent actions to solve their problems, they get into trouble. *Violence* and *anger* are not the same thing. Remember the first list we put on the chalkboard? Look at the words that are circled. Those are examples of *violence*. Violence hurts people. Sometimes violence involves our bodies, but violence can also be words that we use to hurt other people. There are going to be times when you feel angry because a bully is bothering you. It happens to us all. Remember that there are ways to make yourself feel better. Those ways are the items in the second list we wrote on the chalkboard."

Tell the students:

> "I want each of you to think back to the last time you felt angry because someone was bothering you. You don't have to tell about it. I just want you to remember what happened. Remember the feelings you had. Now I want you to think of all the ways we talked about to help yourself deal with those feelings. I am going to give you an activity sheet to help you to remember some of the ways that we talked about for you to work out your anger."

Collect the *Bully-Buster Bingo* game boards and the chips. Distribute *What I Can Do With My Angry Feelings?* and a pencil to each student. Review the directions and tell the students to complete the assignment. When everyone has finished, allow those who wish to do so to share their answers with the group. If you decided to have the students make *Bully-Buster* Folders, tell them to place their activity sheets in their folders. If you are not using folders, allow the students to take their papers home.

Bully-Buster Bingo © 2001 Mar∗co Products, Inc. 1.800.448.2197

WHAT I CAN DO WITH MY ANGRY FEELINGS?

Remember:

It is important to recognize when you are angry and help yourself feel better.

Look at the pictures below. Circle the activities you think might help you deal more successfully with your angry feelings. You may choose more than one activity. If there is something you think would help that is not on the list, write or draw that activity next to *Other Suggestions.*

RUNNING

TAKING A WALK

JUMPING UP AND DOWN

PLAYING A GAME

RIDING A BIKE

TELLING A CARING ADULT

TALKING IT OUT

READING A BOOK

WRITING A LETTER TO THE PERSON I AM ANGRY WITH AND THROWING IT AWAY.

VISITING A FRIEND

WRITING IN A JOURNAL

OTHER SUGGESTIONS:

16

HOW DO I FEEL?
(PRIMARY AND INTERMEDIATE)

RATIONALE: Students need to have an understanding of the messages that their bodies send when they feel threatened. Recognizing these signals can help them remove themselves from stressful environments.

OBJECTIVE: The students will be able to recognize their bodies' reaction to stress, anger, and fear by becoming aware of how they behave in stressful situations.

MATERIALS: For each student:
- [ ] *Bully-Buster Bingo* game board (pages 36-65 or CD)
- [ ] chips
- [ ] copy of *How Do I Feel?* (page 19 or CD)
- [ ] pencil
- [ ] folders (optional)

For the leader:
- [ ] *Bully-Buster Bingo* calling cards
- [ ] chalkboard and chalk

ACTIVITY: Distribute the *Bully-Buster Bingo* game boards and chips. Play a game of *Bully-Buster Bingo*.

Begin the lesson by telling the students:

"Today we are going to talk about what happens to your bodies when you are under stress, such as when you are being picked on or teased by a bully. Can anyone tell me a signal your body might give you when you are feeling upset or scared because a bully is bothering you? *(Accept all answers and write them on the chalkboard.)* That is right. Your body will let you know you're upset by changing in some way. For example, something could happen and you might notice that your face is all scrunched up and you are frowning. When this or other things happen, it is a signal to you that you are afraid or angry. These feelings do not help your body. I am going to draw an outline of a body on the chalkboard. *(Draw an outline of a body.)* Now let's talk about what might happen to each part of the body when you are feeling scared or stressed because someone is bullying you."

Ask the students the following questions. Then write the answers next to the body part you are discussing.

"Let's start with the face. What might happen to your face?" *(tight muscles, red color)*

"What might happen to your neck or back? How might they feel?" *(pain)*

17

"How might you be breathing if you feel that this bully might hurt you?" *(faster, out of breath)*

"Do you think your heart is going to beat faster or more slowly?" *(faster)*

"How do you think your stomach is feeling if you are worried about this bully hurting you?" *(butterfly feelings)*

"What do you think your hands are doing if you are feeling like you might get hurt?" *(clenched)*

"Do you think your legs will be feeling anything different?" *(muscles will tighten, legs will feel like they are pushing into the ground)*

"Will your feet be doing anything to let you know that you need to leave?" *(pointing in the direction you want to walk to)*

Then say:

"Now I am going to erase our make-believe person from the chalkboard. But before I do that, take a good look at him. Does anyone have any questions about how our bodies might send out signals to let us know that we are feeling threatened or in danger—like when a bully is coming after us? *(pause for questions)* Okay, then, I am going to hand out an activity sheet for you to complete."

Collect the *Bully-Buster Bingo* game boards and chips. Distribute *How Do I Feel?* and a pencil to each student. Review the directions and tell the students to complete the assignment. When everyone has finished, allow those who wish to do so to share their answers with the group. If you decided to have the students make *Bully-Buster* Folders, tell them to place their activity sheets in their folders. If you are not using folders, allow the students to take their papers home.

18

HOW DO I FEEL?

REMEMBER: It is important to know how you feel when you are afraid or angry.

Look at the list below. It shows parts of your body where you might feel stress or anger. Circle the words that describe the places in your body where you feel stress. Draw in other arrows and add words if you feel other types of stress in these or in another part of your body that is not mentioned.

REMEMBER: We are all different and we experience stress in different ways!

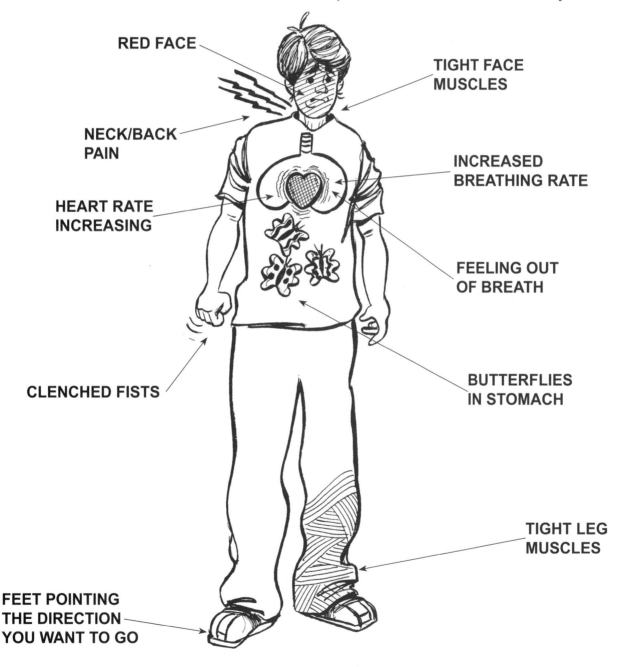

RED FACE

TIGHT FACE
MUSCLES

NECK/BACK
PAIN

INCREASED
BREATHING RATE

HEART RATE
INCREASING

FEELING OUT
OF BREATH

CLENCHED FISTS

BUTTERFLIES
IN STOMACH

TIGHT LEG
MUSCLES

FEET POINTING
THE DIRECTION
YOU WANT TO GO

19

WALKING PROUD
(PRIMARY AND INTERMEDIATE)

RATIONALE: Bullies look for victims. They often decide they will pick on someone almost as soon as they see him/her. A student who walks like someone who will not be intimidated is less likely to become a victim.

OBJECTIVES: The students will identify body postures that help bullies choose their victims.

The students will learn which body postures lessen the likelihood that they'll be singled out as a victim.

MATERIALS: For each student:
- ☐ *Bully-Buster Bingo* game board (pages 36-65 or CD)
- ☐ chips
- ☐ copy of *Walking Proud I and Walking Proud II* (page 22 and 23 or CD)
- ☐ crayons or pencil
- ☐ folders (optional)

For the leader:
- ☐ *Bully-Buster Bingo* calling cards

ACTIVITY: Distribute the *Bully-Buster Bingo* game boards and chips. Play a game of *Bully-Buster Bingo*.

Begin the lesson by telling the students to look at their bingo boards. Ask all the students who have *Walk Proud* on their bingo boards to raise their hands. Then ask the class:

"Why do you believe *Walking Proud* would be included as a way to deal with bullies?" (*Accept all appropriate answers.*)

When the class members realize that their physical posture signals a bully to either use them as a victim or avoid them, distribute *Walking Proud I* and *Walking Proud II* and a pencil or crayons to each student. Review the directions and tell the students to complete the assignment. When everyone has finished, allow those who wish to do so to share their answers with the group.

Ask for volunteers to demonstrate the differences between *walking proud* and *not walking proud.* Then ask for volunteers to demonstrate *walking proud* in a role-play situation. Have the students perform as many role-plays as time will allow.

20

Ask the students:

"When would it be difficult to walk proud? *(When you're frightened and show it, when the bully chases you, etc.)*

Collect the *Bully-Buster Bingo* game boards and chips. If you decided to have the students make *Bully-Buster* Folders, tell them to place their activity sheets in their folders. If you are not using folders, allow the students to take their papers home.

21

WALKING PROUD I

Look at the girl below.
Circle the body parts that would make a bully believe she could be a victim.

22

WALKING PROUD II

Draw a picture of a boy or girl
who knows how to be bully-smart.

Remember all you have learned about how a bully-smart kid walks,
looks straight ahead, holds his/her head high, and walks with confidence.

BULLY BUSTER
(PRIMARY AND INTERMEDIATE)

RATIONALE: Bullies succeed when their victims do not know how to handle the situation. When this happens, the bully is in control. Victims need to know and be able to use different "bully-buster" techniques in order to counteract difficult situations.

OBJECTIVES: The students will identify different "bully-buster" techniques.

The students will role-play different "bully-buster" techniques in typical situations.

MATERIALS: For each student:
- ☐ *Bully-Buster Bingo* game board (pages 36-65 or CD)
- ☐ chips
- ☐ folders (optional)

For each intermediate student group:
- ☐ copy of *Bust The Bullies* (page 27 or CD)
- ☐ pencil

For each intermediate student:
- ☐ copy of *A Bully-Buster Tale* (page 28 or CD)
- ☐ pencil

For the leader:
- ☐ *Bully-Buster Bingo* calling cards
- ☐ overhead projector
- ☐ transparency of *Bully-Buster Techniques* (page 26 or CD)
- ☐ copy of *Bust The Bullies* (page 27 or CD)

ACTIVITY: Distribute the *Bully-Buster Bingo* game boards and chips. Play a game of *Bully-Buster Bingo*.

Begin the lesson by putting the *Bully-Buster Techniques* transparency on the overhead projector. Tell the class:

"This is a list of all the *Bully-Buster Techniques*. Some of them will be on your bingo card. I am going to read each technique and, as I do, I want you to stand if the technique I read appears on your card. I will then ask one of you standing to explain why you believe this technique will work when trying to "bust bullies.""

Read each of the techniques and listen to the students' opinions. Clarify any opinions that may be unclear.

Have the students form small groups or pairs.

If you are working with primary students, read aloud one of the *Bust The Bullies* situations. Tell the students to decide what should be done to "bust the bully" in this situation. Choose one group to role-play its solution. Then discuss the situation and ask other groups to share other possible solutions to the situation. Repeat this process with all of the situations described on the activity sheet.

If you are working with intermediate students, distribute *Bust The Bullies* and a pencil to each group. Tell the students:

> "Read each situation and decide which *Bully-Buster Technique* would work best. Write your choice on the line provided after each situation. Then select one situation that you would like to role-play for the class. You will have (<u>SELECT AN APPROPRIATE TIME ALLOTMENT</u>) to complete this activity."

When the allotted time has elapsed, choose one of the student groups who volunteer to role-play the first situation. Then ask the other student groups if any of them reached a different solution. Allow each student group who elected to role-play the situation and had reached a different solution to role-play its solution to the situation. When all of the players have finished, ask the student groups who have elected to do a different situation to contribute any solutions they reached that are different from the ones already suggested. Continue this process with all the situations on the activity sheet.

If you are working with intermediate students, distribute *A Bully-Buster Tale* and a pencil to each student. Tell the students to finish the story by filling in the blanks. Explain that whatever their solution is, they must be able to give the reason for their choice. Set a time limit, then have the students who wish to do so share their stories with the group. After the stories are shared, discuss the questions at the bottom of the activity sheet.

Collect the *Bully-Buster Bingo* game boards and chips. If you decided to have the students make *Bully-Buster* Folders, tell them to place their activity sheets in their folders. If you are not using folders, allow the students to take their papers home.

BULLY-BUSTER TECHNIQUES

Ignore The Bully
Talk It Out
Answer The Bully With A Firm Voice
Look The Bully Straight In The Eye
Walk Proud
Tell A Caring Adult
Go To A Safe Place
Use "I" Messages
Tell The Bully How You Feel
Avoid Dangerous Areas
Go With Friends
Believe In Yourself
Try Humor
Watch Your Body Language
Walk Away Briskly But Do Not Run
Identify The Bully's Feelings
Remain Calm
Tell Yourself You Can Handle The Situation
Stay Away From Dangerous People
Turn Around And Go Another Way
Get Help
Question The Bully
Don't Lose Your Temper
Agree With Things That Might Be True
Turn Insults Into Compliments
Show Interest In What The Bully Thinks

BUST THE BULLIES

Read each situation carefully. Then, as a group, decide which *Bully-Buster Technique* would be best and write your choice on the line provided. When you have finished, select one situation and be prepared to role-play that situation in front of the class.

SITUATION 1: Walking from the school bus to Bill's front door is a frightening experience every day. Each day, as Bill nears his home, he hopes that the two bullies who hang out about three doors from his house aren't around. When they see him coming, they block the sidewalk so he cannot pass, grab his bookbag, and push him around. They don't hit him. They just bully him until he is ready to cry or scream.

Bill can "bust the bullies" by _____

SITUATION 2: Susan hates to use the girls' bathroom at school because of Jennifer. Whenever the two girls are there at the same time, Jennifer makes fun of Susan. Jennifer tells Susan that none of the other girls like her, that she is dumb, that her clothes look like they have come from a rag bag, or that she is ugly.

Susan can "bust the bully" by _____

SITUATION 3: Mike faces a different threat in the boys' bathroom. He often meets Rick, who threatens to physically hurt Mike if he doesn't hand over part of his lunch money. Since Rick is a lot bigger than Mike, Mike gives him the money.

Mike can "bust the bully" by _____

SITUATION 4: Kelsey is not good at sports. Her class competes with the other grade levels in a physical education day that requires every student to be part of a team. No team wants Kelsey, and when she is placed on a team, the other kids tease her about being no good, about how she'll lose the meet for them, and even suggest that she stay home on the day of the competition.

Kelsey can "bust the bullies" by _____

SITUATION 5: Roberto started a nasty rumor about Juan. Now the other kids are bullying Juan. The rumor is untrue and Juan has tried to tell the kids that what Roberto said is a lie. They don't believe Juan and they keep on bullying him.

Juan can "bust the bullies" by _____

SITUATION 6: Kim and Linda are playing on the swings at a local playground. Three bullies, whom they do not know, tell the girls to get off the swings and "get lost." The bullies are about the same age as Kim and Linda.

Linda and Kim can "bust the bullies" by _____

A BULLY-BUSTER TALE

Read the story and fill in the blanks.

Brenda is in the _____ grade. She has _____ hair and _____ eyes. This is Brenda's first year in _____ School, and things are not going very well for her. Brenda moved from another part of the country and talks differently from the other kids.

Becky is in Brenda's class. She is very popular and has lots of friends. Becky is the leader of her group and she does not like Brenda because_____ . Becky bullies Brenda every chance she gets. She also gets her friends to bully Brenda. When Brenda comes into the classroom, they _____ . In the cafeteria, they _____ . At recess, they _____ . On the school bus, they _____ .

At first, Brenda thought that it was all because she was new. But now she has been in the school for two months and the situation has not improved at all. In fact, it is worse! Brenda _____ to go to school. She feels _____ . Every day, she wishes she were back in her old school with her old friends.

When the bullying began, Brenda tried _____ the girls, but that didn't work. Then she tried_____ , but that did not work, either. As a last resort, she tried _____ . But nothing made the situation better. If anything, it got worse.

Finally Brenda _____ . Becky did not know what to do. She has bullied other people before, but no one had ever _____ . Becky was not a girl who gave up easily. She tried bullying Brenda every chance she had, but Brenda just _____ . What do you think happened next?

Do you think Becky stopped bullying Brenda? _____

When bullying did not work with Brenda, what do you think Becky's friends thought about her?

_____

Do you think Becky would try to bully someone else?_____

28

BULLY LETTER
(INTERMEDIATE)
TO BE WRITTEN AT THE COMPLETION OF UNIT

RATIONALE: Writing this letter allows the students the opportunity to put into practice some of the suggestions that have been introduced in the unit on bullying.

OBJECTIVES: The students will be able to write a letter to a victim, giving advice based on what was taught in the unit on bullying.

The students will write about the importance of telling a trusted adult about what is happening.

MATERIALS: For each student:
- ☐ *Bully-Buster Bingo* game board (pages 36-65 or CD)
- ☐ chips
- ☐ paper
- ☐ pencil
- ☐ folders (optional)

For the leader:
- ☐ *Bully-Buster Bingo* calling cards
- ☐ *Bully Letter* (page 30 or CD)

ACTIVITY: Distribute the *Bully-Buster Bingo* game boards and chips. Play a game of *Bully-Buster Bingo*.

Begin the lesson by telling the students that they will be listening to a letter written by someone their age who is having trouble with a bully. Explain that after they hear the letter, they will be writing a reply. Read the *Bully Letter* aloud to the students. Distribute paper and pencil to the students and allow time for them to answer the letter. Remind them to think of all the bully-buster techniques—especially the importance of telling a caring adult about what is happening—that they have learned from their bingo games and activity sheets and to use their best judgment when answering the letter. Allow the students to use the bully-buster techniques on their bingo game boards for reference.

When everyone has finished, allow those who wish to do so to share their letters. Collect the *Bully-Buster Bingo* game boards. If you decided to have the students make *Bully-Buster* Folders, tell them to place their letters in their folders. If you are not using folders, allow the students to take their papers home.

BULLY LETTER

Dear fellow _____ grader,

I am writing to you today because of a problem that I am having with another student. At recess on the playground the other day, this boy started calling me names.

At first, I tried to ignore him. When he kept calling me names, I tried to avoid him. Then he started to follow me home after school.

Now he says he is going to beat me up! I am really scared and don't know what to do. This boy is really big, and I am afraid I might get hurt.

I don't want to have any problems with him. I am afraid that if I tell my teacher, he will really be after me.

What should I do?

Your friend, I hope,

Bullied at School

BULLYING (A PLAY)
(INTERMEDIATE)

RATIONALE: The play is used to help small groups review the ideas for dealing with bullies that have been discussed.

OBJECTIVES: The students will be able to explain what John and Cathy did wrong and why what they did was wrong.

The students will be able to explain what John and Cathy could have done differently if they had wanted a pencil.

The students will be able to explain what Cathy could have done differently to deal with John's threats.

MATERIALS: For each of the students performing the play:
☐ copy of *Bullying* (pages 33 and 34)

PROCEDURE: (Note: The play should be used in groups of no more than five students who are having problems dealing with other students (friendship groups, anger groups, etc.).

Select the students to play the different parts. Distribute *Bullying* to each student in the play. Then have the students read their parts aloud.

When the play is over ask the students:

"What did John and Cathy do wrong?" *(They stole Mrs. Oaks' pencils.)*

"What could John and Cathy have done differently if they had wanted a pencil?" *(Asked Mrs. Oaks for a pencil and any other appropriate answer.)*

"How could Cathy have dealt differently with John's threats?" *(Refused to be bullied and any other appropriate answer.)*

Tell the students:

"The play you have read is fiction. It did not really happen. But a similar situation could have happened. Tell about a real situation in which you were bullied and then explain what you did and what else you could have done."

When you have finished this activity, ask the students:

"Do you believe you could act differently if you were faced with the same bullying situation again?"

"Do you believe you would be more confident if faced with a bullying situation now than you were before we read the play?"

"If you were involved in a bullying situation, what would you do now that you wouldn't have done before we read the play and had our discussion?"

BULLYING

ACT 1: IN THE CLASSROOM

John: Hey, guys. Look what Mrs. Oaks did. She left her new pencils out on her desk. Let's take them.

Carlos: That's not a good idea, John. You know what happened when we took those erasers. We got in big trouble.

John: That is only because you blabbed to the teacher and confessed. You were a tattletale.

Carlos: Did not!

Cathy: Yes, you did. I remember, Carlos.

Carlos: Fine. Do what you want. I do not want to be involved.

(Carlos leaves.)

John: Carlos is just a big "chicken."

Cathy: Yeah, he sure is.

John: How many pencils are you going to take, Cathy?

Cathy: Me? I'm not going to take any. Mrs. Oaks will tell my parents.

John: So you are "chicken," too?

Cathy: Am not.

John: Yes, you are, if you don't take the pencils. I am going to tell everyone that you are nothing but a "big chicken."

Cathy: No, don't do that. They'll make my life miserable.

John: Okay, then! Let's get them.

(John and Cathy steal the pencils.)

ACT 2: IN THE CLASSROOM

Mrs. Oaks: Has anyone seen my new pencils?

John: Nope.

Cathy: Not me.

Carlos: Yes, you did, Cathy and John. You took them.

Mrs. Oaks: Is this true, Cathy and John?

John: No.

Bully-Buster Bingo © 2001 Mar✳co Products, Inc. 1.800.448.2197

Mrs. Oaks:	John? Remember what we talked about? You were going to always tell the truth.
John:	Yeah, I took a few, but so did Cathy.
Cathy:	You made me!
Mrs. Oaks:	How could John *make* you do anything, Cathy?
Cathy:	Well, he said that if I didn't take the pencils, he would tell everyone that I was a "chicken." I am not a "chicken."
Mrs. Oaks:	That still doesn't explain how John made you steal, Cathy.
Cathy:	Yes it does. If I didn't take those pencils, he'd have told everyone that I was a "chicken." He's done that before, and I didn't want it to happen again.
Mrs. Oaks:	Cathy, did John force your hand to pick up those pencils? Are you a puppet?
Cathy:	No, but …
Mrs. Oaks:	If John didn't force your hand to pick up those pencils, whose decision was it for you to pick them up?
Cathy:	Mine, I guess.
Mrs. Oaks:	You *guess* or you *know*?
Cathy:	I *know*. I made the decision to steal the pencils. Is that what you wanted me to say?
Mrs. Oaks:	It's what I want you to *understand*. We have to accept responsibility for what we do. You decided to take the pencils, just like John did. You are just as guilty. I do understand, Cathy, that you did not want to be called "chicken," but it does not excuse your taking the pencils. (Pause) John, you did two things wrong. Can you tell me what they were?
John:	I took the pencils and I told Cathy I would tell everyone she was "chicken" if she didn't take them, too.
Mrs. Oaks:	That is correct. Is there anything you would like to say to Cathy right now?
John:	Yeah. Cathy, you are not "chicken" and I am sorry I said that to you. (Pause) Mrs. Oaks, what are you going to do to us?
Mrs. Oaks:	I am going to have you write a letter to your parents explaining what you did.
Cathy:	Great, I'll be grounded for a month!
John:	Yeah, I'll be grounded for a year!

Bully-Buster Bingo © 2001 Mar✳co Products, Inc. 1.800.448.2197

BULLYING-BUSTER BINGO

REPRODUCIBLE
GAME BOARDS
CHECK LIST
&
CALLING CARDS

BULLY-BUSTER BINGO

B U L L Y

Ignore The Bully	Talk It Out	Answer The Bully With A Firm Voice	Look The Bully Straight In The Eye	Walk Proud
Tell A Caring Adult	Go To A Safe Place	Use "I" Messages	Tell The Bully How You Feel	Avoid Dangerous Areas
Go With Friends	Believe In Yourself	FREE SPACE	Try Humor	Watch Your Body Language
Walk Away Briskly But Do Not Run	Identify The Bully's Feelings	Remain Calm	Tell Yourself You Can Handle The Situation	Stay Away From Dangerous People
Turn Around And Go Another Way	Get Help	Don't Lose Your Temper	Agree With Things That Might Be True	Turn Insults Into Compliments

BULLY-BUSTER BINGO & ACTIVITIES: CARD #1 © 2001 MAR•CO PRODUCTS, INC. 1.800.448.2197

BULLY-BUSTER BINGO

BULLY

B	U	L	L	Y
Ignore The Bully	Talk It Out	Answer The Bully With A Firm Voice	Look The Bully Straight In The Eye	Walk Proud
Tell A Caring Adult	Go To A Safe Place	Use "I" Messages	Tell The Bully How You Feel	Avoid Dangerous Areas
Go With Friends	Believe In Yourself	FREE SPACE	Try Humor	Watch Your Body Language
Walk Away Briskly But Do Not Run	Identify The Bully's Feelings	Remain Calm	Tell Yourself You Can Handle The Situation	Stay Away From Dangerous People
Turn Around And Go Another Way	Get Help	Don't Lose Your Temper	Agree With Things That Might Be True	Turn Insults Into Compliments

1-2-3-4

BULLY-BUSTER BINGO & ACTIVITIES: CARD #1 © 2001 MAR*CO PRODUCTS, INC. 1.800.448.2197

BULLY-BUSTER BINGO

B U L L Y

B	U	L	L	Y
Tell The Bully How You Feel	Answer The Bully With A Firm Voice	Look The Bully Straight In The Eye	Walk Proud	Tell A Caring Adult
Go To A Safe Place	Use "I" Messages	Talk It Out	Avoid Dangerous Areas	Go With Friends
Believe In Yourself	Try Humor	FREE SPACE	Watch Your Body Language	Walk Away Briskly But Do Not Run
Stay Away From Dangerous People	Remain Calm	Tell Yourself You Can Handle The Situation	Identify The Bully's Feelings	Turn Around And Go Another Way
Get Help	Don't Lose Your Temper	Agree With Things That Might Be True	Turn Insults Into Compliments	Question The Bully

1-2-3-4

BULLY-BUSTER BINGO & ACTIVITIES: CARD #2 © 2001 MAR★CO PRODUCTS, INC. 1.800.448.2197

BULLY-BUSTER BINGO

BULLY

1-2-3-4

B	U	L	L	Y
Answer The Bully With A Firm Voice	Look The Bully Straight In The Eye	Walk Proud	Tell A Caring Adult	Go To A Safe Place
Use "I" Messages	Tell The Bully How You Feel	Don't Lose Your Temper	Go With Friends	Believe In Yourself
Try Humor	Watch Your Body Language	FREE SPACE	Walk Away Briskly But Do Not Run	Identify The Bully's Feelings
Remain Calm	Tell Yourself You Can Handle The Situation	Stay Away From Dangerous People	Turn Around And Go Another Way	Get Help
Avoid Dangerous Areas	Agree With Things That Might Be True	Turn Insults Into Compliments	Question The Bully	Show Interest In What The Bully Thinks

BULLY-BUSTER BINGO

B U L L Y

1-2-3-4

B	U	L	L	Y
Get Help	Walk Proud	Tell A Caring Adult	Go To A Safe Place	Use "I" Messages
Tell The Bully How You Feel	Avoid Dangerous Areas	Go With Friends	Believe In Yourself	Try Humor
Turn Around And Go Another Way	Walk Away Briskly But Do Not Run	**FREE SPACE**	Identify The Bully's Feelings	Remain Calm
Tell Yourself You Can Handle The Situation	Stay Away From Dangerous People	Watch Your Body Language	Look The Bully Straight In The Eye	Don't Lose Your Temper
Agree With Things That Might Be True	Turn Insults Into Compliments	Question The Bully	Show Interest In What The Bully Thinks	Ignore The Bully

BULLY-BUSTER BINGO

BULLY

B	U	L	L	Y
Walk Proud	Tell A Caring Adult	Go To A Safe Place	Use "I" Messages	Tell The Bully How You Feel
Avoid Dangerous Areas	Go With Friends	Walk Away Briskly But Do Not Run	Try Humor	Watch Your Body Language
Believe In Yourself	Identify The Bully's Feelings	FREE SPACE	Remain Calm	Tell Yourself You Can Handle The Situation
Stay Away From Dangerous People	Turn Around And Go Another Way	Get Help	Don't Lose Your Temper	Agree With Things That Might Be True
Turn Insults Into Compliments	Question The Bully	Show Interest In What The Bully Thinks	Ignore The Bully	Talk It Out

1-2-3-4

BULLY-BUSTER BINGO

B U L L Y

1-2-3-4

B	U	L	L	Y
Tell A Caring Adult	Go To A Safe Place	Use "I" Messages	Answer The Bully With A Firm Voice	Avoid Dangerous Areas
Go With Friends	Believe In Yourself	Try Humor	Watch Your Body Language	Walk Away Briskly But Do Not Run
Identify The Bully's Feelings	Remain Calm	FREE SPACE	Tell Yourself You Can Handle The Situation	Stay Away From Dangerous People
Turn Around And Go Another Way	Get Help	Don't Lose Your Temper	Agree With Things That Might Be True	Turn Insults Into Compliments
Question The Bully	Show Interest In What The Bully Thinks	Ignore The Bully	Talk It Out	Tell The Bully How You Feel

BULLY-BUSTER BINGO & ACTIVITIES: CARD #6 © 2001 MAR*CO PRODUCTS, INC. 1.800.448.2197

BULLY-BUSTER BINGO

B U L L Y

B	U	L	L	Y
Go To A Safe Place	Use "I" Messages	Tell The Bully How You Feel	Avoid Dangerous Areas	Go With Friends
Believe In Yourself	Try Humor	Show Interest In What The Bully Thinks	Walk Away Briskly But Do Not Run	Identify The Bully's Feelings
Remain Calm	Tell Yourself You Can Handle The Situation	FREE SPACE	Stay Away From Dangerous People	Turn Around And Go Another Way
Get Help	Don't Lose Your Temper	Agree With Things That Might Be True	Turn Insults Into Compliments	Question The Bully
Watch Your Body Language	Ignore The Bully	Talk It Out	Answer The Bully With A Firm Voice	Look The Bully Straight In The Eye

1-2-3-4

BULLY-BUSTER BINGO & ACTIVITIES: CARD #7 © 2001 MAR*CO PRODUCTS, INC. 1.800.448.2197

BULLY-BUSTER BINGO

B U L L Y

1-2-3-4

B	U	L	L	Y
Use "I" Messages	Tell The Bully How You Feel	Avoid Dangerous Areas	Go With Friends	Believe In Yourself
Try Humor	Watch Your Body Language	Walk Away Briskly But Do Not Run	Identify The Bully's Feelings	Remain Calm
Tell Yourself You Can Handle The Situation	Stay Away From Dangerous People	FREE SPACE	Turn Around And Go Another Way	Get Help
Turn Insults Into Compliments	Agree With Things That Might Be True	Don't Lose Your Temper	Question The Bully	Show Interest In What The Bully Thinks
Ignore The Bully	Talk It Out	Answer The Bully With A Firm Voice	Look The Bully Straight In The Eye	Walk Proud

BULLY-BUSTER BINGO

BULLY

Tell The Bully How You Feel	Avoid Dangerous Areas	Go With Friends	Believe In Yourself	Try Humor
Remain Calm	Walk Away Briskly But Do Not Run	Identify The Bully's Feelings	Watch Your Body Language	Tell Yourself You Can Handle The Situation
Look The Bully Straight In The Eye	Turn Around And Go Another Way	FREE SPACE	Get Help	Don't Lose Your Temper
Agree With Things That Might Be True	Turn Insults Into Compliments	Question The Bully	Show Interest In What The Bully Thinks	Ignore The Bully
Talk It Out	Answer The Bully With A Firm Voice	Stay Away From Dangerous People	Walk Proud	Tell A Caring Adult

1-2-3-4

BULLY-BUSTER BINGO & ACTIVITIES: CARD #9 © 2001 MAR*CO PRODUCTS, INC. 1.800.448.2197

BULLY-BUSTER BINGO

B U L L Y

B	U	L	L	Y
Tell A Caring Adult	Go With Friends	Believe In Yourself	Try Humor	Watch Your Body Language
Walk Away Briskly But Do Not Run	Identify The Bully's Feelings	Remain Calm	Tell Yourself You Can Handle The Situation	Stay Away From Dangerous People
Turn Around And Go Another Way	Get Help	FREE SPACE	Don't Lose Your Temper	Agree With Things That Might Be True
Turn Insults Into Compliments	Question The Bully	Show Interest In What The Bully Thinks	Ignore The Bully	Talk It Out
Answer The Bully With A Firm Voice	Look The Bully Straight In The Eye	Walk Proud	Avoid Dangerous Areas	Go To A Safe Place

1-2-3-4

BULLY-BUSTER BINGO & ACTIVITIES: CARD #10 © 2001 MAR*CO PRODUCTS, INC. 1.800.448.2197

BULLY-BUSTER BINGO

BULLY

B	U	L	L	Y
Go With Friends	Believe In Yourself	Try Humor	Watch Your Body Language	Walk Away Briskly But Do Not Run
Identify The Bully's Feelings	Remain Calm	Tell Yourself You Can Handle The Situation	Stay Away From Dangerous People	Turn Around And Go Another Way
Get Help	Don't Lose Your Temper	FREE SPACE	Agree With Things That Might Be True	Turn Insults Into Compliments
Question The Bully	Show Interest In What The Bully Thinks	Ignore The Bully	Talk It Out	Answer The Bully With A Firm Voice
Look The Bully Straight In The Eye	Walk Proud	Tell A Caring Adult	Go To A Safe Place	Use "I" Messages

1-2-3-4

BULLY-BUSTER BINGO & ACTIVITIES: CARD #11 © 2001 MAR★CO PRODUCTS, INC. 1.800.448.2197

BULLY-BUSTER BINGO

BULLY

1-2-3-4

B	U	L	L	Y
Believe In Yourself	Try Humor	Watch Your Body Language	Walk Away Briskly But Do Not Run	Identify The Bully's Feelings
Remain Calm	Tell Yourself You Can Handle The Situation	Look The Bully Straight In The Eye	Turn Around And Go Another Way	Get Help
Don't Lose Your Temper	Agree With Things That Might Be True	**FREE SPACE**	Turn Insults Into Compliments	Question The Bully
Show Interest In What The Bully Thinks	Ignore The Bully	Talk It Out	Answer The Bully With A Firm Voice	Stay Away From Dangerous People
Walk Proud	Tell A Caring Adult	Go To A Safe Place	Use "I" Messages	Tell The Bully How You Feel

BULLY-BUSTER BINGO

1-2-3-4

B U L L Y

B	U	L	L	Y
Try Humor	Watch Your Body Language	Walk Away Briskly But Do Not Run	Agree With Things That Might Be True	Remain Calm
Tell Yourself You Can Handle The Situation	Stay Away From Dangerous People	Turn Around And Go Another Way	Get Help	Answer The Bully With A Firm Voice
Identify The Bully's Feelings	Turn Insults Into Compliments	FREE SPACE	Question The Bully	Show Interest In What The Bully Thinks
Ignore The Bully	Talk It Out	Don't Lose Your Temper	Look The Bully Straight In The Eye	Walk Proud
Tell A Caring Adult	Go To A Safe Place	Use "I" Messages	Tell The Bully How You Feel	Avoid Dangerous Areas

*BULLY-BUSTER BINGO & ACTIVITIES: CARD #13© 2001 MAR*CO PRODUCTS, INC. 1.800.448.2197*

BULLY-BUSTER BINGO

B U L L Y

B	U	L	L	Y
Watch Your Body Language	Walk Away Briskly But Do Not Run	Identify The Bully's Feelings	Remain Calm	Tell A Caring Adult
Stay Away From Dangerous People	Turn Around And Go Another Way	Get Help	Don't Lose Your Temper	Agree With Things That Might Be True
Turn Insults Into Compliments	Question The Bully	**FREE SPACE**	Show Interest In What The Bully Thinks	Ignore The Bully
Talk It Out	Answer The Bully With A Firm Voice	Go To A Safe Place	Walk Proud	Tell Yourself You Can Handle The Situation
Look The Bully Straight In The Eye	Use "I" Messages	Tell The Bully How You Feel	Avoid Dangerous Areas	Go With Friends

1-2-3-4

BULLY-BUSTER BINGO & ACTIVITIES: CARD #14 © 2001 MAR*CO PRODUCTS, INC. 1.800.448.2197

BULLY

1-2-3-4

B	U	L	L	Y
Walk Away Briskly But Do Not Run	Identify The Bully's Feelings	Remain Calm	Tell Yourself You Can Handle The Situation	Go To A Safe Place
Turn Around And Go Another Way	Get Help	Question The Bully	Agree With Things That Might Be True	Turn Insults Into Compliments
Don't Lose Your Temper	Show Interest In What The Bully Thinks	FREE SPACE	Ignore The Bully	Talk It Out
Answer The Bully With A Firm Voice	Look The Bully Straight In The Eye	Walk Proud	Tell A Caring Adult	Stay Away From Dangerous People
Use "I" Messages	Tell The Bully How You Feel	Avoid Dangerous Areas	Go With Friends	Believe In Yourself

BULLY-BUSTER BINGO & ACTIVITIES: CARD #15 © 2001 MAR✶CO PRODUCTS, INC. 1.800.448.2197

1-2-3-4

BULLY

B	U	L	L	Y
Identify The Bully's Feelings	Remain Calm	Tell Yourself You Can Handle The Situation	Stay Away From Dangerous People	Turn Around And Go Another Way
Get Help	Don't Lose Your Temper	Try Humor	Turn Insults Into Compliments	Question The Bully
Show Interest In What The Bully Thinks	Ignore The Bully	**FREE SPACE**	Talk It Out	Answer The Bully With A Firm Voice
Look The Bully Straight In The Eye	Tell A Caring Adult	Walk Proud	Go To A Safe Place	Use "I" Messages
Tell The Bully How You Feel	Avoid Dangerous Areas	Go With Friends	Believe In Yourself	Agree With Things That Might Be True

BULLY-BUSTER BINGO & ACTIVITIES: CARD #16 © 2001 MAR*CO PRODUCTS, INC. 1.800.448.2197

BULLY-BUSTER BINGO

1-2-3-4

B U L L Y

B	U	L	L	Y
Remain Calm	Tell Yourself You Can Handle The Situation	Don't Lose Your Temper	Turn Around And Go Another Way	Get Help
Stay Away From Dangerous People	Agree With Things That Might Be True	Turn Insults Into Compliments	Question The Bully	Show Interest In What The Bully Thinks
Ignore The Bully	Talk It Out	FREE SPACE	Answer The Bully With A Firm Voice	Look The Bully Straight In The Eye
Walk Proud	Tell A Caring Adult	Go To A Safe Place	Tell The Bully How You Feel	Use "I" Messages
Avoid Dangerous Areas	Go With Friends	Believe In Yourself	Try Humor	Watch Your Body Language

BULLY-BUSTER BINGO & ACTIVITIES: CARD #17© 2001 MAR*CO PRODUCTS, INC. 1.800.448.2197

BULLY-BUSTER BINGO

BULLY

B	U	L	L	Y
Tell Yourself You Can Handle The Situation	Stay Away From Dangerous People	Ignore The Bully	Turn Around And Go Another Way	Don't Lose Your Temper
Agree With Things That Might Be True	Turn Insults Into Compliments	Question The Bully	Show Interest In What The Bully Thinks	Get Help
Talk It Out	Answer The Bully With A Firm Voice	FREE SPACE	Look The Bully Straight In The Eye	Walk Proud
Tell A Caring Adult	Go To A Safe Place	Use "I" Messages	Tell The Bully How You Feel	Avoid Dangerous Areas
Watch Your Body Language	Believe In Yourself	Try Humor	Go With Friends	Walk Away Briskly But Do Not Run

1-2-3-4

BULLY-BUSTER BINGO

BULLY

B	U	L	L	Y
Stay Away From Dangerous People	Turn Around And Go Another Way	Get Help	Don't Lose Your Temper	Talk It Out
Turn Insults Into Compliments	Question The Bully	Agree With Things That Might Be True	Ignore The Bully	Show Interest In What The Bully Thinks
Answer The Bully With A Firm Voice	Look The Bully Straight In The Eye	FREE SPACE	Walk Proud	Tell A Caring Adult
Go To A Safe Place	Use "I" Messages	Tell The Bully How You Feel	Avoid Dangerous Areas	Go With Friends
Believe In Yourself	Watch Your Body Language	Try Humor	Walk Away Briskly But Do Not Run	Identify The Bully's Feelings

BULLY-BUSTER BINGO

B U L L Y

B	U	L	L	Y
Turn Around And Go Another Way	Get Help	Use "I" Messages	Agree With Things That Might Be True	Turn Insults Into Compliments
Tell A Caring Adult	Show Interest In What The Bully Thinks	Ignore The Bully	Talk It Out	Answer The Bully With A Firm Voice
Look The Bully Straight In The Eye	Walk Proud	FREE SPACE	Question The Bully	Go To A Safe Place
Don't Lose Your Temper	Tell The Bully How You Feel	Avoid Dangerous Areas	Go With Friends	Believe In Yourself
Try Humor	Watch Your Body Language	Walk Away Briskly But Do Not Run	Identify The Bully's Feelings	Remain Calm

BULLY-BUSTER BINGO

BULLY

B	U	L	L	Y
Get Help	Don't Lose Your Temper	Agree With Things That Might Be True	Turn Insults Into Compliments	Question The Bully
Show Interest In What The Bully Thinks	Ignore The Bully	Look The Bully Straight In The Eye	Answer The Bully With A Firm Voice	Go With Friends
Walk Proud	Tell A Caring Adult	FREE SPACE	Go To A Safe Place	Use "I" Messages
Tell The Bully How You Feel	Avoid Dangerous Areas	Remain Calm	Believe In Yourself	Try Humor
Watch Your Body Language	Walk Away Briskly But Do Not Run	Identify The Bully's Feelings	Tell Yourself You Can Handle The Situation	Talk It Out

BULLY-BUSTER BINGO

BULLY

B	U	L	L	Y
Don't Lose Your Temper	Agree With Things That Might Be True	Turn Insults Into Compliments	Question The Bully	Show Interest In What The Bully Thinks
Ignore The Bully	Talk It Out	Answer The Bully With A Firm Voice	Tell The Bully How You Feel	Walk Proud
Tell A Caring Adult	Go To A Safe Place	FREE SPACE	Use "I" Messages	Look The Bully Straight In The Eye
Avoid Dangerous Areas	Go With Friends	Believe In Yourself	Try Humor	Watch Your Body Language
Remain Calm	Identify The Bully's Feelings	Walk Away Briskly But Do Not Run	Tell Yourself You Can Handle The Situation	Stay Away From Dangerous People

1·2·3·4

BULLY-BUSTER BINGO & ACTIVITIES: CARD #22 © 2001 MAR*CO PRODUCTS, INC. 1.800.448.2197

BULLY-BUSTER BINGO

BULLY

B	U	L	L	Y
Agree With Things That Might Be True	Turn Insults Into Compliments	Question The Bully	Show Interest In What The Bully Thinks	Ignore The Bully
Talk It Out	Answer The Bully With A Firm Voice	Remain Calm	Walk Proud	Tell A Caring Adult
Go To A Safe Place	Use "I" Messages	FREE SPACE	Tell The Bully How You Feel	Avoid Dangerous Areas
Go With Friends	Believe In Yourself	Try Humor	Walk Away Briskly But Do Not Run	Watch Your Body Language
Identify The Bully's Feelings	Look The Bully Straight In The Eye	Tell Yourself You Can Handle The Situation	Stay Away From Dangerous People	Turn Around And Go Another Way

1-2-3-4

BULLY-BUSTER BINGO

BULLY

B	U	L	L	Y
Use "I" Messages	Question The Bully	Show Interest In What The Bully Thinks	Ignore The Bully	Walk Proud
Answer The Bully With A Firm Voice	Look The Bully Straight In The Eye	Talk It Out	Tell A Caring Adult	Go To A Safe Place
Walk Away Briskly But Do Not Run	Tell The Bully How You Feel	FREE SPACE	Avoid Dangerous Areas	Go With Friends
Believe In Yourself	Try Humor	Watch Your Body Language	Turn Insults Into Compliments	Identify The Bully's Feelings
Remain Calm	Tell Yourself You Can Handle The Situation	Get Help	Turn Around And Go Another Way	Stay Away From Dangerous People

1-2-3-4

BULLY-BUSTER BINGO & ACTIVITIES: CARD #24 © 2001 MAR*CO PRODUCTS, INC. 1.800.448.2197

BULLY

B	U	L	L	Y
Question The Bully	Show Interest In What The Bully Thinks	Look The Bully Straight In The Eye	Talk It Out	Answer The Bully With A Firm Voice
Ignore The Bully	Walk Proud	Tell A Caring Adult	Go To A Safe Place	Use "I" Messages
Tell The Bully How You Feel	Avoid Dangerous Areas	**FREE SPACE**	Go With Friends	Believe In Yourself
Try Humor	Watch Your Body Language	Don't Lose Your Temper	Identify The Bully's Feelings	Remain Calm
Tell Yourself You Can Handle The Situation	Stay Away From Dangerous People	Turn Around And Go Another Way	Get Help	Walk Away Briskly But Do Not Run

1-2-3-4

BULLY-BUSTER BINGO

B U L L Y

B	U	L	L	Y
Show Interest In What The Bully Thinks	Ignore The Bully	Watch Your Body Language	Answer The Bully With A Firm Voice	Tell The Bully How You Feel
Walk Proud	Tell A Caring Adult	Go To A Safe Place	Use "I" Messages	Look The Bully Straight In The Eye
Avoid Dangerous Areas	Go With Friends	FREE SPACE	Agree With Things That Might Be True	Try Humor
Get Help	Walk Away Briskly But Do Not Run	Identify The Bully's Feelings	Remain Calm	Tell Yourself You Can Handle The Situation
Stay Away From Dangerous People	Talk It Out	Turn Around And Go Another Way	Don't Lose Your Temper	Believe In Yourself

1-2-3-4

BULLY-BUSTER BINGO & ACTIVITIES: CARD #26 © 2001 MAR*CO PRODUCTS, INC. 1.800.448.2197

BULLY-BUSTER BINGO

B U L L Y

B	U	L	L	Y
Remain Calm	Talk It Out	Walk Proud	Look The Bully Straight In The Eye	Get Help
Tell A Caring Adult	Go To A Safe Place	Use "I" Messages	Tell The Bully How You Feel	Avoid Dangerous Areas
Don't Lose Your Temper	Believe In Yourself	FREE SPACE	Try Humor	Answer The Bully With A Firm Voice
Tell Yourself You Can Handle The Situation	Identify The Bully's Feelings	Ignore The Bully	Go With Friends	Stay Away From Dangerous People
Watch Your Body Language	Walk Away Briskly But Do Not Run	Turn Around And Go Another Way	Agree With Things That Might Be True	Turn Insults Into Compliments

BULLY-BUSTER BINGO & ACTIVITIES: CARD #27 © 2001 MAR*CO PRODUCTS, INC. 1.800.448.2197

1-2-3-4

BULLY-BUSTER BINGO

BULLY

1-2-3-4

B	U	L	L	Y
Use "I" Messages	Talk It Out	Answer The Bully With A Firm Voice	Look The Bully Straight In The Eye	Walk Away Briskly But Do Not Run
Tell A Caring Adult	Walk Proud	Identify The Bully's Feelings	Believe In Yourself	Remain Calm
Go With Friends	Tell The Bully How You Feel	FREE SPACE	Turn Insults Into Compliments	Watch Your Body Language
Agree With Things That Might Be True	Try Humor	Get Help	Show Interest In What The Bully Thinks	Stay Away From Dangerous People
Turn Around And Go Another Way	Avoid Dangerous Areas	Don't Lose Your Temper	Ignore The Bully	Question The Bully

BULLY-BUSTER BINGO & ACTIVITIES: CARD #28 © 2001 MAR*CO PRODUCTS, INC. 1.800.448.2197

BULLY-BUSTER BINGO

BULLY

B	U	L	L	Y
Try Humor	Walk Proud	Tell A Caring Adult	Stay Away From Dangerous People	Use "I" Messages
Believe In Yourself	Avoid Dangerous Areas	Look The Bully Straight In The Eye	Walk Away Briskly But Do Not Run	Agree With Things That Might Be True
Watch Your Body Language	Show Interest In What The Bully Thinks	FREE SPACE	Identify The Bully's Feelings	Remain Calm
Tell Yourself You Can Handle The Situation	Don't Lose Your Temper	Turn Around And Go Another Way	Tell The Bully How You Feel	Go With Friends
Go To A Safe Place	Turn Insults Into Compliments	Question The Bully	Get Help	Ignore The Bully

1-2-3-4

BULLY-BUSTER BINGO & ACTIVITIES: CARD #29 © 2001 MAR*CO PRODUCTS, INC. 1.800.448.2197

BULLY-BUSTER BINGO

B U L L Y

B	U	L	L	Y
Show Interest In What The Bully Thinks	Avoid Dangerous Areas	Tell Yourself You Can Handle The Situation	Believe In Yourself	Try Humor
Tell The Bully How You Feel	Walk Away Briskly But Do Not Run	Identify The Bully's Feelings	Remain Calm	Answer The Bully With A Firm Voice
Stay Away From Dangerous People	Turn Around And Go Another Way	FREE SPACE	Get Help	Don't Lose Your Temper
Agree With Things That Might Be True	Go With Friends	Question The Bully	Ignore The Bully	Turn Insults Into Compliments
Talk It Out	Walk Proud	Look The Bully Straight In The Eye	Watch Your Body Language	Tell A Caring Adult

1-2-3-4

BULLY-BUSTER BINGO & ACTIVITIES: CARD #30 © 2001 MAR*CO PRODUCTS, INC. 1.800.448.2197

REPRODUCIBLE BULLY-BUSTER BINGO CHECKLIST

B

- [ ] Agree With Things That Might Be True
- [ ] Answer The Bully With A Firm Voice
- [ ] Avoid Dangerous Areas
- [ ] Believe In Yourself
- [ ] Don't Lose Your Temper
- [ ] Get Help
- [ ] Go To A Safe Place
- [ ] Go With Friends
- [ ] Identify The Bully's Feelings
- [ ] Ignore The Bully
- [ ] Look The Bully Straight In The Eye
- [ ] Question The Bully
- [ ] Remain Calm
- [ ] Show Interest In What The Bully Thinks
- [ ] Stay Away From Dangerous People
- [ ] Talk It Out
- [ ] Tell A Caring Adult
- [ ] Tell The Bully How You Feel
- [ ] Tell Yourself You Can Handle The Situation
- [ ] Try Humor
- [ ] Turn Around And Go Another Way
- [ ] Turn Insults Into Compliments
- [ ] Use "I" Messages
- [ ] Watch Your Body Language
- [ ] Walk Away Briskly But Do Not Run
- [ ] Walk Proud

U

- [ ] Agree With Things That Might Be True
- [ ] Answer The Bully With A Firm Voice
- [ ] Avoid Dangerous Areas
- [ ] Believe In Yourself
- [ ] Don't Lose Your Temper
- [ ] Get Help
- [ ] Go To A Safe Place
- [ ] Go With Friends
- [ ] Identify The Bully's Feelings
- [ ] Ignore The Bully
- [ ] Look The Bully Straight In The Eye
- [ ] Question The Bully
- [ ] Remain Calm
- [ ] Show Interest In What The Bully Thinks
- [ ] Stay Away From Dangerous People
- [ ] Talk It Out
- [ ] Tell A Caring Adult
- [ ] Tell The Bully How You Feel
- [ ] Tell Yourself You Can Handle The Situation
- [ ] Try Humor
- [ ] Turn Around And Go Another Way
- [ ] Turn Insults Into Compliments
- [ ] Use "I" Messages
- [ ] Watch Your Body Language
- [ ] Walk Away Briskly But Do Not Run
- [ ] Walk Proud

L

- [ ] Agree With Things That Might Be True
- [ ] Answer The Bully With A Firm Voice
- [ ] Avoid Dangerous Areas
- [ ] Believe In Yourself
- [ ] Don't Lose Your Temper
- [ ] Get Help
- [ ] Go To A Safe Place
- [ ] Go With Friends
- [ ] Identify The Bully's Feelings
- [ ] Ignore The Bully
- [ ] Look The Bully Straight In The Eye
- [ ] Question The Bully
- [ ] Remain Calm
- [ ] Show Interest In What The Bully Thinks
- [ ] Stay Away From Dangerous People
- [ ] Talk It Out
- [ ] Tell A Caring Adult
- [ ] Tell The Bully How You Feel
- [ ] Tell Yourself You Can Handle The Situation
- [ ] Try Humor
- [ ] Turn Around And Go Another Way
- [ ] Turn Insults Into Compliments
- [ ] Use "I" Messages
- [ ] Watch Your Body Language
- [ ] Walk Away Briskly But Do Not Run
- [ ] Walk Proud

Y

- [ ] Agree With Things That Might Be True
- [ ] Answer The Bully With A Firm Voice
- [ ] Avoid Dangerous Areas
- [ ] Believe In Yourself
- [ ] Don't Lose Your Temper
- [ ] Get Help
- [ ] Go To A Safe Place
- [ ] Go With Friends
- [ ] Identify The Bully's Feelings
- [ ] Ignore The Bully
- [ ] Look The Bully Straight In The Eye
- [ ] Question The Bully
- [ ] Remain Calm
- [ ] Show Interest In What The Bully Thinks
- [ ] Stay Away From Dangerous People
- [ ] Talk It Out
- [ ] Tell A Caring Adult
- [ ] Tell The Bully How You Feel
- [ ] Tell Yourself You Can Handle The Situation
- [ ] Try Humor
- [ ] Turn Around And Go Another Way
- [ ] Turn Insults Into Compliments
- [ ] Use "I" Messages
- [ ] Watch Your Body Language
- [ ] Walk Away Briskly But Do Not Run
- [ ] Walk Proud

Bully-Buster Bingo © 2001 Mar*co Products, Inc. 1.800.448.2197

B Ignore The Bully © 2001 MAR∗CO PRODUCTS, INC.	**B** Talk It Out © 2001 MAR∗CO PRODUCTS, INC.	**B** Look The Bully Straight In The Eye © 2001 MAR∗CO PRODUCTS, INC.
B Walk Proud © 2001 MAR∗CO PRODUCTS, INC.	**B** Tell A Caring Adult © 2001 MAR∗CO PRODUCTS, INC.	**B** Answer The Bully With A Firm Voice © 2001 MAR∗CO PRODUCTS, INC.
B Use "I" Messages © 2001 MAR∗CO PRODUCTS, INC.		

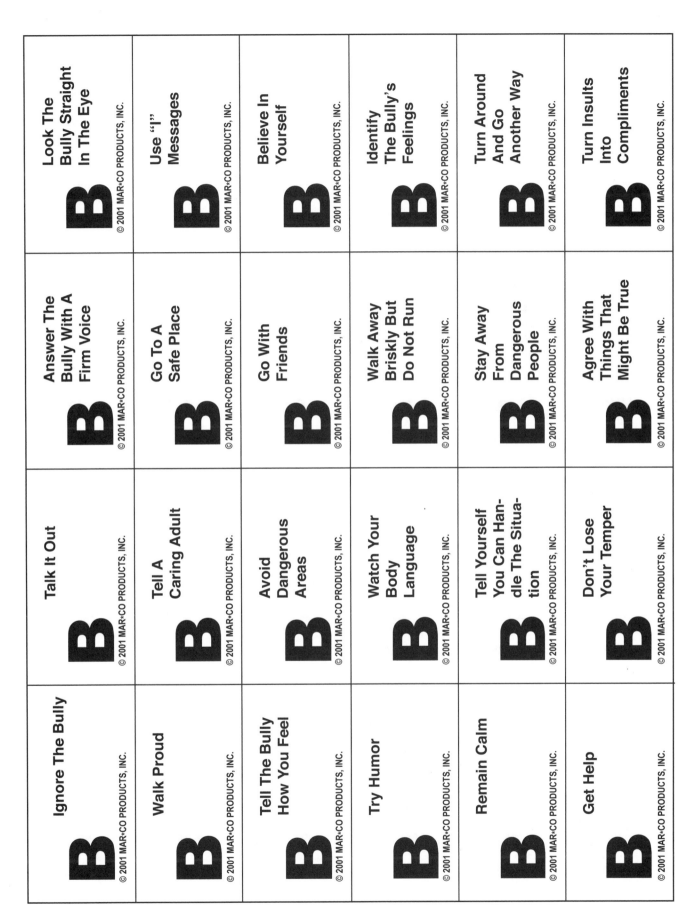

B Tell The Bully How You Feel © 2001 MAR∗CO PRODUCTS, INC.	**B** Avoid Dangerous Areas © 2001 MAR∗CO PRODUCTS, INC.	**B** Go To A Safe Place © 2001 MAR∗CO PRODUCTS, INC.
B Try Humor © 2001 MAR∗CO PRODUCTS, INC.	**B** Watch Your Body Language © 2001 MAR∗CO PRODUCTS, INC.	**B** Go With Friends © 2001 MAR∗CO PRODUCTS, INC.
		B Believe In Yourself © 2001 MAR∗CO PRODUCTS, INC.
B Remain Calm © 2001 MAR∗CO PRODUCTS, INC.	**B** Tell Yourself You Can Handle The Situation © 2001 MAR∗CO PRODUCTS, INC.	**B** Walk Away Briskly But Do Not Run © 2001 MAR∗CO PRODUCTS, INC.
		B Identify The Bully's Feelings © 2001 MAR∗CO PRODUCTS, INC.
		B Stay Away From Dangerous People © 2001 MAR∗CO PRODUCTS, INC.
B Get Help © 2001 MAR∗CO PRODUCTS, INC.	**B** Don't Lose Your Temper © 2001 MAR∗CO PRODUCTS, INC.	**B** Turn Around And Go Another Way © 2001 MAR∗CO PRODUCTS, INC.
		B Agree With Things That Might Be True © 2001 MAR∗CO PRODUCTS, INC.
		B Turn Insults Into Compliments © 2001 MAR∗CO PRODUCTS, INC.

Ignore The Bully © 2001 MAR*CO PRODUCTS, INC.	Talk It Out © 2001 MAR*CO PRODUCTS, INC.	Look The Bully Straight In The Eye © 2001 MAR*CO PRODUCTS, INC.
Walk Proud © 2001 MAR*CO PRODUCTS, INC.	Tell A Caring Adult © 2001 MAR*CO PRODUCTS, INC.	Use "I" Messages © 2001 MAR*CO PRODUCTS, INC.
Answer The Bully With A Firm Voice © 2001 MAR*CO PRODUCTS, INC.	Go To A Safe Place © 2001 MAR*CO PRODUCTS, INC.	Believe In Yourself © 2001 MAR*CO PRODUCTS, INC.
Tell The Bully How You Feel © 2001 MAR*CO PRODUCTS, INC.	Avoid Dangerous Areas © 2001 MAR*CO PRODUCTS, INC.	Go With Friends © 2001 MAR*CO PRODUCTS, INC.
Try Humor © 2001 MAR*CO PRODUCTS, INC.	Watch Your Body Language © 2001 MAR*CO PRODUCTS, INC.	Walk Away Briskly But Do Not Run © 2001 MAR*CO PRODUCTS, INC.
Identify The Bully's Feelings © 2001 MAR*CO PRODUCTS, INC.	Tell Yourself You Can Han-dle The Situa-tion © 2001 MAR*CO PRODUCTS, INC.	Stay Away From Dangerous People © 2001 MAR*CO PRODUCTS, INC.
Turn Around And Go Another Way © 2001 MAR*CO PRODUCTS, INC.	Remain Calm © 2001 MAR*CO PRODUCTS, INC.	Don't Lose Your Temper © 2001 MAR*CO PRODUCTS, INC.
Agree With Things That Might Be True © 2001 MAR*CO PRODUCTS, INC.	Get Help © 2001 MAR*CO PRODUCTS, INC.	Turn Insults Into Compliments © 2001 MAR*CO PRODUCTS, INC.

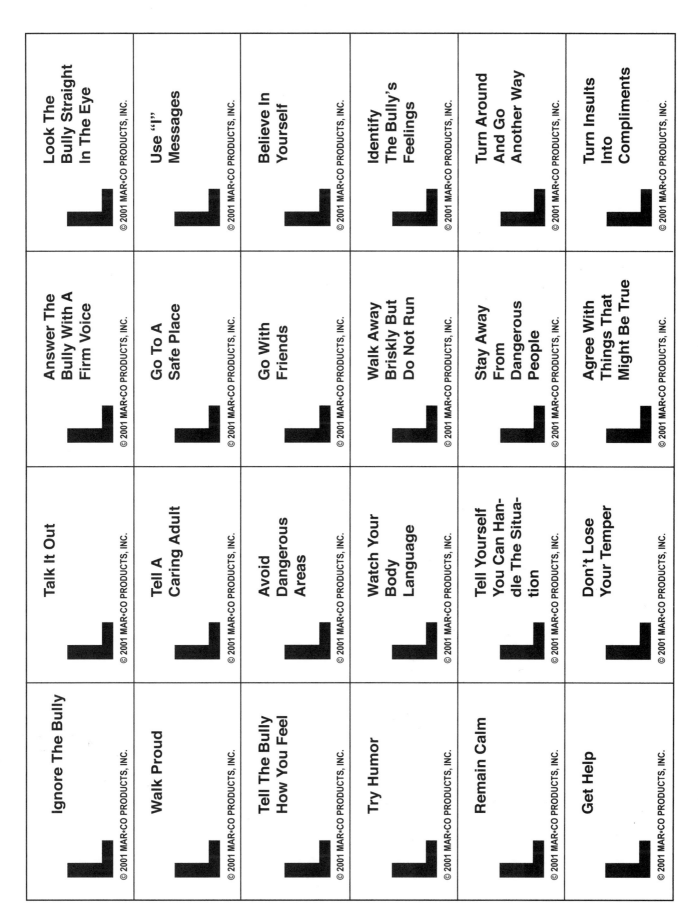

Ignore The Bully © 2001 MAR*CO PRODUCTS, INC.	Talk It Out © 2001 MAR*CO PRODUCTS, INC.	Answer The Bully With A Firm Voice © 2001 MAR*CO PRODUCTS, INC.	Look The Bully Straight In The Eye © 2001 MAR*CO PRODUCTS, INC.
Walk Proud © 2001 MAR*CO PRODUCTS, INC.	Tell A Caring Adult © 2001 MAR*CO PRODUCTS, INC.	Go To A Safe Place © 2001 MAR*CO PRODUCTS, INC.	Use "I" Messages © 2001 MAR*CO PRODUCTS, INC.
Tell The Bully How You Feel © 2001 MAR*CO PRODUCTS, INC.	Avoid Dangerous Areas © 2001 MAR*CO PRODUCTS, INC.	Go With Friends © 2001 MAR*CO PRODUCTS, INC.	Believe In Yourself © 2001 MAR*CO PRODUCTS, INC.
Try Humor © 2001 MAR*CO PRODUCTS, INC.	Watch Your Body Language © 2001 MAR*CO PRODUCTS, INC.	Walk Away Briskly But Do Not Run © 2001 MAR*CO PRODUCTS, INC.	Identify The Bully's Feelings © 2001 MAR*CO PRODUCTS, INC.
Remain Calm © 2001 MAR*CO PRODUCTS, INC.	Tell Yourself You Can Handle The Situation © 2001 MAR*CO PRODUCTS, INC.	Stay Away From Dangerous People © 2001 MAR*CO PRODUCTS, INC.	Turn Around And Go Another Way © 2001 MAR*CO PRODUCTS, INC.
Get Help © 2001 MAR*CO PRODUCTS, INC.	Don't Lose Your Temper © 2001 MAR*CO PRODUCTS, INC.	Agree With Things That Might Be True © 2001 MAR*CO PRODUCTS, INC.	Turn Insults Into Compliments © 2001 MAR*CO PRODUCTS, INC.

Look The Bully Straight In The Eye	Answer The Bully With A Firm Voice	Talk It Out	Ignore The Bully
© 2001 MAR*CO PRODUCTS, INC.	© 2001 MAR*CO PRODUCTS, INC.	© 2001 MAR*CO PRODUCTS, INC.	© 2001 MAR*CO PRODUCTS, INC.
Use "I" Messages	Go To A Safe Place	Tell A Caring Adult	Walk Proud
© 2001 MAR*CO PRODUCTS, INC.	© 2001 MAR*CO PRODUCTS, INC.	© 2001 MAR*CO PRODUCTS, INC.	© 2001 MAR*CO PRODUCTS, INC.
Believe In Yourself	Go With Friends	Avoid Dangerous Areas	Tell The Bully How You Feel
© 2001 MAR*CO PRODUCTS, INC.	© 2001 MAR*CO PRODUCTS, INC.	© 2001 MAR*CO PRODUCTS, INC.	© 2001 MAR*CO PRODUCTS, INC.
Identify The Bully's Feelings	Walk Away Briskly But Do Not Run	Watch Your Body Language	Try Humor
© 2001 MAR*CO PRODUCTS, INC.	© 2001 MAR*CO PRODUCTS, INC.	© 2001 MAR*CO PRODUCTS, INC.	© 2001 MAR*CO PRODUCTS, INC.
Turn Around And Go Another Way	Stay Away From Dangerous People	Tell Yourself You Can Handle The Situation	Remain Calm
© 2001 MAR*CO PRODUCTS, INC.	© 2001 MAR*CO PRODUCTS, INC.	© 2001 MAR*CO PRODUCTS, INC.	© 2001 MAR*CO PRODUCTS, INC.
Turn Insults Into Compliments	Agree With Things That Might Be True	Don't Lose Your Temper	Get Help
© 2001 MAR*CO PRODUCTS, INC.	© 2001 MAR*CO PRODUCTS, INC.	© 2001 MAR*CO PRODUCTS, INC.	© 2001 MAR*CO PRODUCTS, INC.

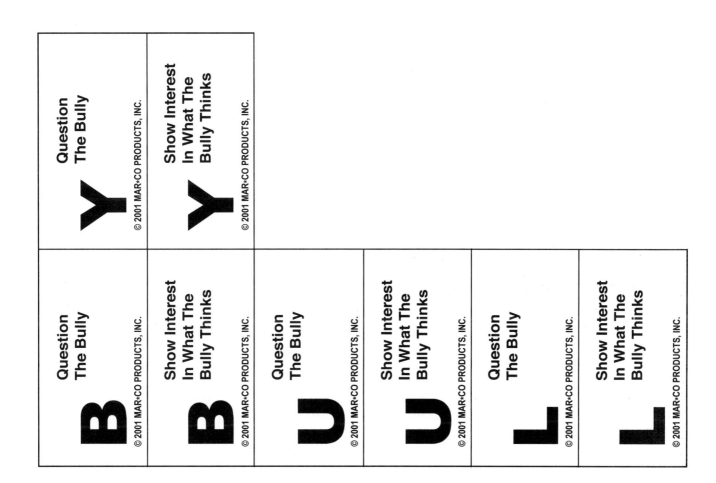

B
Question
The Bully

© 2001 MAR*CO PRODUCTS, INC.

B
Show Interest
In What The
Bully Thinks

© 2001 MAR*CO PRODUCTS, INC.

U
Question
The Bully

© 2001 MAR*CO PRODUCTS, INC.

U
Show Interest
In What The
Bully Thinks

© 2001 MAR*CO PRODUCTS, INC.

L
Question
The Bully

© 2001 MAR*CO PRODUCTS, INC.

L
Show Interest
In What The
Bully Thinks

© 2001 MAR*CO PRODUCTS, INC.

Y
Question
The Bully

© 2001 MAR*CO PRODUCTS, INC.

Y
Show Interest
In What The
Bully Thinks

© 2001 MAR*CO PRODUCTS, INC.

Instructions For Using The CD

The CD found inside the back cover provides ADOBE® PDF files of each lesson's reproducible pages and the bingo game boards, checklist, and calling cards.

Some of the activity pages and the bingo boards are provided in both color and black and white. These pages may be printed in color or black and white. Choose the appropriate setting on your computer.

These files cannot be modified/edited.

System requirements to open PDF (.pdf) files:

Adobe Reader® 5.0 or newer (compatible with Windows 2000® or newer or Mac OS 9.0® or newer).

THIS CD MAY NOT BE DUPLICATED OR DISTRIBUTED.

PERMISSION TO REPRODUCE: The purchaser may reproduce the PDF files, free and without special permission, for participant use for a particular group or class. Reproduction of these materials for an entire school system is forbidden.